Social Anxiety Control for Teens

A CBT Guide to Feel Comfortable and Build Social Confidence Skills

By

Estelle Guzman

TSB Publications

About the Author

Estelle Guzman is an expert clinical psychologist and cognitive behavioral therapist for anxiety and depression. He has extensive research work in clinical psychology and helps children, teens, and children with self-awareness, self-compassion, behavioral, and mindfulness-based techniques. Estelle Guzman also assists people in overcoming fear-based beliefs. He has almost fifteen years of expertise in his field. He has worked with teenagers suffering from chronic stress, anxiety, depression, and emotional dysregulation. Estelle Guzman is aware of the helplessness of raising an anxious teen and wants to use his professional experience to assist more teens and parents in a similar situation.

Table of contents

Introduction

Socially anxious teens experience anxiety during social interactions since almost everyone gets apprehensive when they start a discussion with someone they do not know or ask a question in class. Some teenagers have severe social anxiety that makes them avoid social interactions. This book will help you if you feel your anxiety is pulling the wrong strings.

Fear is a healthy and helpful emotion. It is essential for human survival since it helps us fight for our lives or flee from danger fast. But excessive fear, as manifested in persistent anxiety, is excruciatingly uncomfortable and crippling. Anxiety is a constant fear that lasts after an actual threat has passed when there is no real risk present or before a potential future threat. Anxiety disorders develop when anxiety takes over your life and becomes persistent.

The most effective treatment for anxiety is cognitive behavioral therapy (CBT). It performs better than all the other methods to manage anxiety. There are essentially two CBT methods for treating anxiety: coping and exposure. Coping involves altering your way of thinking, appropriately assessing hazards, and increasing your confidence in your capacity to handle a situation so that you become progressively less fearful. Exposure is the deliberate way of what you are scared of to disprove your dreadful catastrophe predictions until your anxiety naturally fades.

The most recent research indicates that both methods are helpful, although exposure can be more effective and provide more significant, longer-lasting decreases in anxiety. Consider all the things you can accomplish after your anxiety fades! Read this book, then apply its advice. Your confidence is about to emerge.

The second part of this book is where you will outline various strategies for ending your safety-focused habits and exposing yourself to the circumstances, emotions, and ideas you have been avoiding. You will forecast the worst-case scenario for each exposure you have planned and provide a probability that the scenario will materialize.

You might unwind and feel confident and at ease—as you likely imagine everyone else does. Unfortunately, worry cannot entirely be eliminated because it is a trait of the human condition and affects everyone.

You are aware that life is about more than merely surviving. Your aspirations for the future and your ideal way of living are held within your heart. The fundamental tenet of this entire book is that your life is not in your control. You can control your life the more adept you get at distinguishing between the real you and that anxious you. You will learn to track your social anxiety in the book's first part and become conscious of how it causes your uncomfortable feelings and avoidance. The second part is about building willingness and ability to cope with your social anxiety.

Note to Grown Ups

It is a self-help book for teens. It defines social anxiety and offers advice on overcoming it so you can pursue your goals in life. However, self-help is not always sufficient. Helping your kid or finding a therapist to work with may be necessary if your child is struggling to overcome social anxiety or doing the exercises in this book. Still, they do not appear to be helping. It resembles learning a sport in specific ways. You might still need a coach if you read the game's rules and what you need to practice to improve.

Similar to coaches are grown-ups and therapists. They can help you build the necessary skills and identify things, including safe habits, that teens might not be aware of. Additionally, they could inspire teens to proceed with challenging exposures. Cognitive behavioral therapy (CBT) lies at the center of this book. The link between thoughts (cognitions), feelings, and action is a critical component of CBT. A CBT therapist will assist your child in recognizing and challenging the ideas that are increasing their anxiety and changing the behaviors that exacerbate their issue. All anxiety disorders, including social anxiety, can be effectively treated with CBT. Finding a therapist trained in CBT is crucial if you decide to seek treatment for your teen.

Part 1: Let's Track Your Social Anxiety

As teens, experiencing social anxiety is common. However, many social issues disappear over time and with practice. The actual test is not whether you experience anxiety in a circumstance but rather whether you try to prevent it or not. Avoiding circumstances that make you uncomfortable is one way to manage social anxiety, but if that worked for you, you would not be reading this book. That is not the right way to handle your social anxiety.

The fundamental tenet of cognitive therapy is that how we think affects how we feel, how we act, and even how our bodies respond to our environment. In other words, circumstances do not elicit certain emotions or reactions from you. How you feel or act in any case depends on how you understand it. Therefore, even if a circumstance may seem upsetting, your thoughts about the event are the source of your distress. So, if you want to alter your response, begin by altering your thought process. So, before guiding you to change your thought process and handle your social anxiety, I want you to track and find the origin of your anxiety.

Jack's Story: Why are People Staring at Me?

Jack was trapped in this constant thought. Jack had been extroverted and self-assured up until high school when he began to experience social anxiety and self-consciousness. One of his pals once made fun of him in front of the whole class. Jack experienced embarrassment and humiliation. Following that, he began to consider his words more before speaking them. He was cautious to avoid offending anyone in casual talks. He became increasingly quiet and lost behind in talks because he had to consider every word he said carefully.

Jack experiences embarrassment, humiliation, and shame due to his social anxiety, which is the dread of doing or doing anything that will make people laugh at him or reject him. One in twenty adults and teens experience social anxiety, the most prevalent type. Some teenagers with social anxiety have always been reserved; others, like Jack, were extroverted as youngsters but developed social anxiety in middle or high school.

There is a Threat

Teenagers today seek to blend in. But, if your peers reject you, there will be a price. Happiness and well-being depend on relationships with others and yourself too. Therefore, a little anxiety is normal. But what if, like Jack:

+ You constantly worry about "messing up."
+ You feel like you are on stage, in the spotlight, performing for a highly critical audience everywhere you go.
+ You feel that every word you say or your actions are being scrutinized.

Social anxiety can severely hamper your social, career, and academic life. Your nervous system is responding to threats to your safety just as intended. You are not in danger; that is the only difference. However, your social anxiety is raising the alarm. Its purpose is to keep you safe, and if your peers did not like you, that would be dangerous from the "keep it safe" perspective.

If you relate to Jack, you are on the right track to understanding and overcoming your social anxiety. However, you see anything less than complete acceptance as a threat. That threat says that if one person finds one thing boring, everyone may find everything you sound boring.

Your thoughts exaggerate the danger that you will be judged harshly to the point that you will become an outcast. If someone did judge you badly, it understates your capacity to handle it. One worrying thought follows another. These are the kinds of ideas that lead to the avoidant conduct that all anxiety disorders involve. Avoiding circumstances that make you anxious is only natural. Still, by doing so, you instruct your mind to think that its wild assumptions about fictitious threats are accurate and encourage it to invent more of them.

Jack avoided his friends' potential criticism by remaining silent during chats with his classmates. If he genuinely believed he had anything to say, he practiced it word-for-word first to ensure he would not make any mistakes. Jack managed to stay away from the threat by avoiding spontaneity. Nevertheless, he was caught in a 'There is a threat" pattern. He was unhappy that his world was getting smaller and smaller.

Why am I Anxious?

You require anxiety as a strategy for survival. Anxiety serves the same purpose as a smoke alarm in a home to warn us of danger. However, if you are a socially nervous teen, your internal smoke detector goes off whenever someone cooks something. Why, then, is it that your smoke detector is so sensitive while others are not?

There are the following causes of social anxiety. But, as you will see, none of them is your fault:

+ Your social anxiety might be because of your genetics. This quality was not something you came up with on your own. Instead, you might find someone in your family who exhibits worrisome attributes similar to yours. They might not have experienced full-blown social anxiety, but you might have noticed that they had it. Identify any of your family members that you know to be socially anxious.

+ Your parents' role modeling may have influenced your social anxiety if they are highly cautious or shy

+ Almost everyone has forgotten their lines during a presentation in school. While most people can laugh about the incident, socially anxious persons may view it as a catastrophe. Being called upon in class or giving an oral presentation makes them physically ill because they are so afraid of repeating their performance.

Giving the incorrect answer in class, learning that you were not invited to a party while everyone else was, hearing a rumor that you liked a classmate you did not, or being ridiculed in front of the class by a cruel instructor could all have been your unique traumatic incident.

Put it in Writing

Do you have any relatives who suffered from social anxiety?
Yes/No

Do your parents socialize infrequently?
Yes/No

What distressing incidents come to mind while being among people?

_____

_____

_____

Unfortunately, the past cannot be changed. Therefore, your distressing experiences, parental influences, and genetic make-up will always be a part of you. The remedy is the same regardless of the root of your social anxiety. You can control your thoughts and anxiety.

Choosing Avoidance as a Safety

What sort of behaviors are safe? All of us are predisposed to defend ourselves in difficult situations. We will take swift action and take considerable measures to feel safe when we perceive a threat. For example, if you hear footsteps behind you in a dark parking garage, you would probably move quickly to get into your car for protection. You will find yourself looking for safety to escape the anxiety you feel when you worry about something and look for safety in response to a physically hazardous situation.

Safety behaviors are deliberate acts you take to shield yourself from the fear, emotion and disasters you worry about. Safety practices are appealing because they yield quick advantages. They temporarily lessen the sense of danger. For instance, accepting an invitation to eat out can make you anxious about being exposed to the crowd, the chairs, and the public bathrooms. You will feel better immediately if you say no to the invitation and stay away from the restaurant and all of the supposed dangers that go along with it.

If you decide to go, you might adopt safety behaviors and measures. Engaging in these safety practices reduces your concerns due to your lack of action to lessen the fear. However, your fear of crowds directly will likely persist and even worsen. Safety behaviors come in two forms: avoidance and approach. When you engage in avoidant safety behaviors, you avoid, postpone, or flee the fear. You experience an instant reduction in anxiety when you engage in this coping strategy, which makes it incredibly appealing.

With approach safety behaviors, you participate in the anxiety-inducing circumstance while implementing preventative or mitigating measures for your feared outcomes. You feel better immediately if you engage in either of these safety behaviors. What, then, is the issue with them? Utilizing safety behaviors has the drawback that you never learn anything. You never find out if your dreaded event or circumstance can harm you. You never develop the capacity for uncertainty and confidence in your judgment. As a result, whenever the same threat reappears in the future, you experience the same level of fear and manage it by taking the same precautions.

Anxiety tends to increase in frequency and intensity, not decrease, as you continue to repeat the same cycle. Avoidance is the major one, the single most crucial safety behavior, and the primary source of concern. Removing yourself from an unclear or dangerous situation might lessen anxiety by avoiding what you fear. Avoid circumstances when you have to interact with strangers. You could put off obtaining your yearly physical because you fear what the doctor might say. If a task or challenge makes you fear failure or danger, you might avoid it.

Situational, cognitive, and sensation or interoceptive avoidance are the three types of avoidant safety behaviors that people adopt to try to reduce their anxiety.

Put a checkmark next to the type(s) of avoidance you have employed as you read the descriptions below. Do not give up if you utilize all three; it is not uncommon for teens to do so.

No matter what avoidance techniques you employ, this method will be helpful to you.

Situational Avoidance: It is the most typical kind of avoidance. You avoid things, people, places, and activities that make you anxious.

Mary's Situational Avoidance

For instance, Mary once attempted to pet a dog when it nipped her hand. Nevertheless, Mary's aversion to dogs persisted. She avoided parks and other outdoor locations where dogs were permitted as an adult and refused to attend any gatherings at the homes of friends who had dogs. Mary could escape the emotions brought on when she was around dogs in the short term, but she missed out on encounters with friends and loved ones for a long time.

Cognitive avoidance is a particular form of avoidance that only occurs in your head. Your deliberate efforts to repress painful thoughts or upset memories require significant work. This could entail changing them out for more enjoyment or diverting things like fantasies, mantras, daydreams, prayers, or other thinking rituals. Alternately, you can attempt using drugs, risky behaviors, self-harm, binge eating, and other things to numb painful thoughts.

Jerry's Cognitive Avoidance

For instance, Jerry found it challenging to ignore memories of being molested by a neighbor when he was a child. He tried to avoid that trauma through some risky behaviors. He also shied away from sexual activities that brought back memories of the molestation. He tried to suppress the recollections, but they persisted, along with thoughts of being wicked and wrong. Jerry's cognitive avoidance not only failed to prevent anxiety but also led to a social retreat, a breakup with his partner, and depression—a sense that he was failing at life.

Interoceptive Avoidance

Your efforts are concentrated on avoiding internal feelings like feeling heated, weary, difficult breathing, or a rapid heartbeat when you engage in sensation avoidance, also known as interoceptive avoidance. Even if they feel similar to anxiety symptoms, enjoyable experiences like sexual arousal or eagerness for an event may be avoided.

Ellen's Interoceptive Avoidance

Ellen, for instance, experienced a manic episode. She experienced palpitations, a panic attack, and palsy that left her "completely out of it." She has been afraid and keeps eyeing any of these feelings. She furiously tries to block or stop them, staying away from potential hot spots. Ellen, as a result, has stopped exercising altogether to prevent experiencing heart palpitations, becoming hot, or becoming overly aroused.

She does not go on hikes, watch sports, go to concerts, or hang out with pals. Even worse, Ellen starts to feel lightheaded and "out of it" if she suspects she might panic, which frequently sets off a full-blown attack.

You might discover that you can disassemble some of the goods in your list into multiple parts after concentrating on the different sorts of avoidance.

For instance, the following things could make someone afraid:

- Crowded places
- Bustling restaurants
- Cinemas
- Shopping centers
- Nightclubs
- Supermarket

Distorted Thoughts

You might think of anxiety as a lens that distorts your thoughts and how you see the world. Any positive aspects of your life are obscured by your anxiety lens, which restricts your perspective of potentially positive outcomes, brings the negative into great focus, and magnifies any threats you may face. Misappraisal is an inaccurate or skewed evaluation of a threat or danger. You set yourself up for ongoing anxiety when you continuously overestimate the level of threat you are encountering. Three unfavorable thought patterns or ways of perceiving the world that distorts reality are the root of all false threat assessments.

The three distorted thought patterns that make up the anxiety lens are as follows:

+ Negative Focus

  - My life is full of problems.
  - His lack of empathy is intolerable to me.

+ Negative Predictions

  - I am not going to complete this assignment in time.
  - I am going to lose him.

+ Problem Exaggeration

  - My anxiety will kill me.
  - It is not feasible.

The reality is your thoughts are distorting there. You might not see the distortion and accept those ideas as accurate, which only serves to increase your level of fear. When aware of their distortion, taking your thoughts less seriously is simpler.

Here are those distortions that people with social anxiety make:

Thinking Catastrophically

What is the worst that can happen? You adopt catastrophic thinking when a trigger situation arises, and your mind automatically assumes the worst-case scenario, despite having a hundred other conceivable outcomes.

Emily's Story of Thinking Catastrophically

Will I be accepted into a good college? So it was Emily's story. She had submitted all her college applications but had not heard back from anyone. Many of her friends have already received acceptance, but not her, making her anxious. She believed that she might not be accepted. Her thoughts looked like this: What will I do if I am turned away? Maybe I am not talented or intelligent enough.

When presented with uncertainty, Emily projected the worst-case scenario and allowed catastrophizing to make that image into an even more terrible nightmare. In this instance, she assumed that she would never be accepted into the college of her choice or, worse still, that she would not be admitted after hearing others discuss being accepted. As a result, Emily panics rather than maintain her optimism or speak with her college advisor.

Your Turn

Give an example of a time in your life when you exhibited catastrophic thinking.

_____

_____

_____

What was the worst thing you could have imagined happening?

_____

_____

_____

Undervaluing the Positive

Do you attribute luck when nice things occur to you? Do you assume someone who compliments you was just trying to be nice? Imagine conversing with someone and, rather than being completely speechless, you found the conversation enjoyable. You conclude, "Well, he is very nice, and that's why I felt comfortable, but most people are not like that, and I would freeze up talking with them," rather than feeling glad that sometimes you genuinely do have anything to talk about. Minimizing your accomplishments and successes makes it challenging to grow confident.

Put it in Writing

Has somebody ever complimented you and did not think you deserved it?

_____

_____

_____

How did you take the compliment lightly?

_____

_____

_____

You might be aware of everything with all your senses engaged, yet you ignore all the positive information in favor of the negative. What circumstances allow you to focus solely on what is not working?

Labeling

While words can hurt you seriously, sticks and stones will still break your bones. You are demeaning someone else if you call them names. Self-labeling lowers your self-esteem. For instance, you tell yourself you are a loser after dropping your books in the hallway. But we have all made careless errors. Are we all so dull? You are not an idiot if you just yell forth a stupid idea. Labels like "lame," "loser," and "idiot" do not fully capture who you are. Socially anxious teens frequently use these types of labels to describe themselves. You use which on yourself.

Spotlighting

We experience self-consciousness when we put ourselves in the center of attention. What ought to be a free-flowing and natural expression of oneself turns into a painful performance. Being highlighted makes you feel unique and alienated from other people. Your every word begins to seem strange or artificial. You do not like or trust how you come across; to make matters worse, you believe that everyone is watching you just as intently as you are.

When you are focused on what is happening inside yourself, how can you connect with others and get into the flow of life? Everyone experiences self-consciousness, but most people are aware of it and move on. They flip a switch, extinguishing the light. However, socially anxious teenagers turn up the spotlight when they feel self-conscious, which makes them so aware of themselves that they become paralyzed. You can draw attention to what is happening inside your body.

These common anxiety symptoms will worsen if you concentrate on something else while shivering, blushing, or sweating. For instance, you might notice your heart pumping quickly while speaking in class. Then, as you pay attention to your heartbeat, the hammering gets worse to the point where it feels like your heart would burst into flames.

You tell yourself, "Everyone around me can see what is happening."

"They are aware of my panic!"

After class, the spotlight follows you out of the room, illuminating your ungainly gait for everyone to see. When you are living in the spotlight, this is how the day goes.

Put it in Writing

Describe a circumstance in which you felt like the center of attention.

_____

_____

_____

What impression do you think you gave to others?

_____

_____

_____

What emotions do you feel the people around you must witness?

_____

_____

_____

Read My Mind

It is normal for you to fear that everyone is thinking about you if you feel like you are in the spotlight and everyone is watching you. Being a mind reader makes you think you know what other people think, especially when they say negative things about you. Despite not possessing any psychic abilities, you somehow just know. And since you are so confident, you do not care to investigate what is happening. For instance, your friend with whom you are hanging out suddenly starts to get preoccupied. You can read minds. Therefore, you know your companion was seeking an out since she was bored and wanted to leave.

Put it in Writing

Describe an incident where you met someone and felt nervous.

_____

_____

_____

What did you believe they were contemplating about you?

_____

_____

_____

Perfectionism

The social perfectionist has two possible outcomes: you are brilliant, intelligent, famous, dull, boring, and an outcast. There is no such thing as okay or sufficient. Nobody likes you if you are not invited to every party. If people are not listening intently, you are bored whenever you open your lips to speak. When everyone's constant approval of you defines normal for you, you have set the bar too high and will never achieve it. Nobody is socially flawless, and trying to be one will only make you feel ashamed. There is no room for error under social perfectionism. Although it is a harsh method to evaluate oneself, it is the most pervasive misperception and the worst for shy teenagers.

Teens question their abilities in friendships and romantic relationships. They experience misery after being rejected or going through a breakup, and even the most self-assured people can have uncertainty when pursuing new relationships. It is inevitable to encounter challenging or unpleasant social settings. Everyone will occasionally experience anxiety. But by developing the ability to notice your uncertainty and replace it with confidence, you may reduce challenges, unpleasant feelings, and poor decisions.

Albert's Story of Perfectionism

Albert was concerned with what others would think. He kept trying different outfits from his closet until he found the ideal outfit. He told him that he was not attractive. People would not like him if he did not look good.

Why is Albert such a stickler for his appearance and every action he takes? This insecurity is a result of very high expectations creating doubt distortion. He also overestimates the significance of his beauty as a result of chasing perfectionism. Albert also worried he would be late for everything because he struggles with decision-making.

Looking at friendships through the prism of anxiety and self-doubt can become a painful strain. Self-criticism follows doubt because we feel we have failed and been rejected. As a result, we allow our insecurities to dominate how we view ourselves and our interpersonal interactions. However, friendships do not have to be a source of anxiety and worry. You would not perceive criticism that is not there when you feel you are a nice person and can therefore approach relationships with self-confidence.

When you solely think about your flaws, pursuing relationships can be unsettling and cause anxiety. Doubt makes you accentuate and concentrate on the worst parts of who you are or a scenario. You acquire the big view and the strength to pursue your goals when you convince yourself to see the benefits.

Acceptance: Free Yourself

Acceptance sets us free. Have you ever gone on hiking? A high trail rapidly makes you exhausted. You soon start to sweat and feel worn out. The path zigzags, and a fresh section of rugged terrain is revealed with each abrupt turn. You cannot see what is up ahead because of the trees, and you start to doubt your ability to reach the summit. It is so tempting to turn around. You become increasingly exhausted to the point where you can hardly put one foot in front of the other. You arrive at the peak!

As the path progresses, so does your exhaustion. Your body feels exhausted, and your legs are unsteady, yet you also feel fantastic. You triumphed over the mountain. Fatigue is like anxiety. If you decide to face your fear, it will grow worse before it gets better, just like choosing to climb a mountain. But remember, you do not trek up the hill complaining about being exhausted! It is unacceptable to be worn out! If you had that thinking, you would undoubtedly turn around and return to the bottom.

You accept your tiredness since you know it comes with climbing a challenging trail. You are aware of and have faith that if you take breaks and catch your breath at each bend, your exhaustion will not kill you, and you will eventually find the energy to complete your task. Accepting anxiety as a natural aspect of life makes it much easier to deal with.

Your ability to embrace what the new environment offers will determine your success when you consider it. That includes your physical tiredness when out on the trail. It contains the worry you will experience on your ladder. You will embrace that anxiousness as it appears.

Embrace the Moment

The decision to accept uneasiness would not be sufficient. You will need to embrace it fully in the areas of your body where you experience anxiety. You have historically breathed quickly and shallowly when anxious, which is a fight-or-flight reaction. Breathe in, fill your lungs with air, so your belly grows. Then exhale. Reiterate carefully and purposefully. Not that difficult, is it? It might be straightforward, but it is also clearly effective.

The fight-or-flight responses in your body are countered and softened by breathing into fear. Your body is instructed to breathe quickly and shallowly by your inner cries, but you override that order by taking deep, deliberate breaths. Here is a piece of advice: Do not attempt to unwind. You will need to be fully present in the scenario, precisely like in the mindfulness practice, feeling every moment thoroughly, for your challenges to be successful and aid you in achieving your objective. It is okay if you chance to become relaxed while accepting your nervous feelings with your breath; it is also okay if you become more anxious. As long as you embrace your fear and breathe through your worry, you rise to the occasion and move up the ladder.

Anxiety has a start, middle, and end, just like everything else in the natural world. Now try this experiment:

Imagine a scenario, scene, or idea that gives you pause. Whenever you experience that sensation in your body, breathe into it without trying to change anything. Keep doing this while paying great attention to your physical sensations. You will notice that your level of anxiety is shifting. It might become stronger or weaker, and your body could be moved by it. Everything is alright.

You can lessen your resistance to anxiety by breathing through it and letting it proceed naturally. You might be surprised by how effectively your body can deal with negative emotions. You would not lose your balance, get dizzy, or have a heart attack. You are considerably more potent than your monkey believes! But, naturally, it would not be simple.

You can change your situation, regardless of how deeply ingrained your avoidance pattern is. You will be able to recognize the beast for what it is with acceptance and confidence. Why do I sound so sure of myself? Because the same forces that made the anxiety grow will also make it shrink. Your anxious mind cannot take credit for your success when you avoid a crisis and manage to endure it. You survived because it ended up being a tolerable problem. Although it was terrifying, you made it through, and by doing so, you gained confidence in your capacity to handle anxiety and accomplish what you needed.

The chatter of your anxious mind will become less enticing as you come to terms with the fact that fear is merely an emotion and not necessarily a warning that something is wrong. Your thoughts will change from I feel uneasy; I should leave this area so I can be in this scenario even though I feel anxious. By steadily advancing up your ladder one step at a time, envision all the activities you will engage in and the locations you will visit.

Part 2: Building Willingness and Ability to Cope with Social Anxiety

Feeling comfortable with yourself and building comfortable social skills depend on one's ability to develop the willingness and cope with social anxiety. Anyone can build self-confidence. To achieve this, focus on the facts and objectively examine your circumstances. This enables you to identify and dismantle your erroneous and biased thoughts. You may objectively assess your thinking and recognize how doubt might taint your self-view and worldview now that you know how to record and examine your thoughts. You may overcome doubt with action, time and practice, and you will develop a fresh, self-assured, and accurate picture of yourself. In this chapter, I will teach you to build those abilities.

Road to Exposure

Exposures do not always turn out as expected. You prepared for and were excited to expose yourself to your fears, but once you were there, you had far more anxiety than anticipated. You fled as your avoidance instinct took over. Now what? If you cannot think of anything lower, try thinking creatively to see if you can.

For instance, Isabella, who considered herself boring, intended to go to lunch with a few friends and discuss things she did over the weekend. She did go with her friends, but when it was her turn to speak, she began to sweat and worried that it would seem strange to start talking exclusively about herself. Before the exposure, she had assumed this would be very simple and had nothing else on her ladder. So Isabella thought of two ways to lower it for the next time:

+ She might alter the circumstance by selecting people with whom she felt more at ease or conversing with one person instead of two.
+ She might alter her course of action by answering two questions — which was easier for her to do — and giving just one instance of her weekend activities.

Keep in mind that feeling worried is very normal. In reality, if you are incredibly nervous, you have chosen something that needs serious improvement. But, at least you have that to look forward to. It is also typical that as you practice exposure, your anxiety will decrease, and your confidence will increase. Get a coach; occasionally, having a friend or parent help you with your direction can be helpful. Even just telling someone your plans can help you follow through.

You might be able to get someone to accompany you, depending on how exposed you are. However, you still experience the same anxiety when traveling on the road to exposure for the tenth time as you did the first time. Repeated exposures typically result in a decrease in pressure, even if it is only a minor one. Understandably, it can be discouraging when this does not occur.

Consider what might hold you back before you give up and start avoiding that circumstance again. Take a close look at your exposure strategy since you might not be aware of it even if you were doing it. Are you defending yourself from an embarrassing outcome in any way? You will not get the benefits if you navigate the issue without taking any real risks.

Keep in mind that safe practices are like water wings. You are in the water, and you think the fact that you are wearing them is the only thing keeping you from drowning. However, if you do not have to kick and paddle to stay afloat, your fear of the water will not disappear.

Perhaps you are using your distorted thoughts, the warped ways of thinking. They give you a false impression of who you are and how the world is. You could find it challenging to get into the swing of things since you are so self-conscious and conscious of everything you say and do. To avoid making a mistake, you pay close attention to yourself. Try removing yourself from the spotlight.

Allow yourself to speak without restraint. Pay close attention to the people and surroundings you are in. Also, watch out for unfavorable biases when you are paying attention. Teens who struggle with social anxiety often overlook the good things around them and overreact to the bad. Do you constantly scrutinize your face for boredom, disappointment, disgust, or irritability? Teens who experience anxiety frequently interpret others' harmless facial expressions as being judgmental.

Many teenagers believe that they can get by on their own, that everything is obvious, and that taking notes wastes time. You are more likely to revert to your previous habitual ideas and safety behaviors if you perform exposures without putting them in writing. Without spending the time to complete the written part, you are also more likely to become fixated on failing to achieve a perfectionist objective and less likely to view the experience in a new light, which entails moving in the direction of your values and fulfilling your priorities.

Journaling the exposure can be a good experiment. Start with your anxieties and deceptions. Spend time considering each question and provide the most truthful response possible. Making an honest evaluation of your unproductive thoughts, aspirations, and behaviors is essential before you can come up with new ones. What can you tell yourself to keep you from running away when things get difficult? Always keep in mind what you can genuinely accomplish and the reason you are doing this.

Did you complete it? Great! Tell a dependable friend or an understanding parent about it. Like tests, exposures can yield better results with better preparation. Do not forget to complete the postexposure evaluation once you have done an exposure. Your responses to these queries will aid your recovery if you believe the exposure went poorly. Conversely, your responses will assist in establishing the following step on your ladder if you think the exposure went well. Journaling your way through your concerns can feel awkward and tiresome, especially before you start reaping the benefits of your efforts.

As you acquire momentum and approach your goals, you will begin to comprehend your worry differently. You will learn to lean into your fear as opposed to fighting it. After each exposure, try answering these questions as honestly as possible:

Did you meet your realistic goal regarding your exposure?

_____

_____

_____

Did you use avoidance as a safety? Or did you face your fears?

_____

_____

_____

What was the result?

_____

_____

_____

What did you learn?

_____

_____

_____

Your Thoughts Create Your Reality

Ever try to block out thoughts of something? It does not have to be a word—it might be any word—but let's try it with "school" for the sake of argument. Do not think about a school for the next one minute. How did you find that to work? The truth is that attempting to drive thoughts out of our minds would not work; it can make them recur more frequently. Usually, changes in our experiences lead to changes in how we think. But if you continue to trust your recurring fearful ideas, it is unlikely that you will encounter any novel situations.

Your thoughts create your reality. Therefore, if you want to attempt new things, gain fresh experience, and develop in the direction of your ideals, you must confront your anxious thoughts. You must do this by probing them with logical inquiries rather than by blocking or eliminating them.

Let's look at Noah's thoughts while meeting his friend.

Noah's anxiety said: "I do not know what to say."

Perfectionism says: I would not have anything to say. My friend is going to think I am weird.

Labeling said: "Does not say something clever that is equal to being weird? If I humiliate myself in front of him, he will tell all his friends how weird I am, and then the entire school will think I am weird."

A negative mindset said: "The worst will happen. How was I supposed to handle that?

He hardly recognized him when he met his friend and just said hello.

Your coping ideas are formed through the responses to challenging questions.

Let's look at some of Noah's questions and his coping strategies:

1. Do I know for sure that I would not have anything to say?

His Copying Strategy: "I might be able to come up with something to say. I believe I can greet him with a smile."

2. Does not expressing something clever equal being odd?

His Copying Strategy: "I do not think people are weird when they do not know what to say. He might not believe I am strange either."

3. What is most likely to happen? How was I supposed to handle that?

His Copying Strategy: "He might not even glance at me. He may put on a nasty and arrogant act. If it were to occur, I could discuss it with a buddy and, at the very least, would know he was not the one for me."

After he went and met his friend, his question was:

"What did I do that was okay."

He said to himself, "I was assertive. I approached him directly and greeted him. I gave myself the evidence I needed to confirm my courage. As a result, he is now aware of my existence, and I have an opportunity to get to know him better."

Now it is your turn to answer those questions based on one of your personal worry-related experiences.

Use questions as you see fit.

Which scenario is more likely to occur? How would I handle it?

_____

_____

_____

What did I do that was acceptable?

_____

_____

_____

What else would everyone be focusing on but me, I wondered? Do people genuinely care about what I do that much?

_____

_____

_____

According to mind reading, what proof do I have that people think this way?

_____

_____

_____

Do I demand more of myself than I do of others? Recall your thinking, emotion, and action.

_____

_____

_____

You have an alternative to your long-standing automatic nervous thoughts with each new coping strategy you develop. Coping mechanisms will enable you to face your anxieties, exposing you to novel experiences that will lead to fresh perspectives.

Facing Fear

A deceptively straightforward two-step procedure can be used to summarize the anxiety solution: abstain from your typical behavior or try something you usually avoid. You will finally confront and conquer your fear in this chapter, turning off your previous false alarms. It is difficult to face something you think will probably cause you damage. The only way to overcome anxiety permanently is to confront your fears. Untreated anxiety problems typically worsen over time. Fear increasingly limits and closes in on life as avoidance breeds further avoidance.

Everything you do to feel safer only serves to temporarily calm you before the next wave of fear overcomes you. Without contradictory experiences, you cannot change your conviction that something will hurt you. It is challenging and brave, but it will set you free.

Jordan's Story of Facing His Fear

Jordan's mind is stuck in this thought: "I will freak out speaking in front of the class." The teacher just informed the class that an oral presentation is one of the requirements on the first day of class. I am panicked and very freaked out. I think I will do a lousy job. I will embarrass myself. I will be too nervous about doing it."

Nervousness is an expression of fear. Jordan's dread originates from believing he is facing a difficult situation unprepared. It is the extreme thinking mixed with the uncertainty distortion of future projections. Jordan sees his oral presentation in a threatening way. He worries that he might make a mistake and look foolish.

Here are some perspectives that could help Jordan get off the path of self-doubt and face his fear:

Instead of worrying, consider all the times you have spoken in front of a group of students. No matter what happens, it will not be the disaster you imagine. Often, facing a dreaded situation is the best way to dispute your fear. Building up your resources gives you the tools you need to handle any situation, threat or not. Consider it from various perspectives, and you can overcome your fears by understanding that everyone else must do it.

Your ability to believe in yourself is your most valuable asset. Here is what Jordan thinks of when he switches his give-up thoughts for go-to ideas:

- If you know your material and are prepared, you can do this. What could go wrong? You are nervous and stumble over a word — no big deal. Being confident means not making this into more than it is. Just the mandatory oral presentation is involved.

- Put the danger into perspective. Any fear or threat will be lowered if you have confidence in your abilities. How anxious you do not define the outcome.

Breaking the Bubble of Perfectionism

I will exhort you to break your bubble of perfectionism. You might ask a dumb question or irritate someone. It is not quite as absurd as it seems. Remember that your attempts to stop negative things from happening led you down the avoidance path. You have undoubtedly likely felt some embarrassment from your exposures so far.

In reality, you have probably learned that you are stronger than you initially thought, and you have learned a few coping mechanisms. Imagine how effective your coping mechanisms would be if you deliberately used them to make your fearful predictions come true. For example, a skater once said, "If you are not falling, you are not skating." This means genuine skaters always push themselves beyond their comfort zones by attempting new moves and higher jumps. To improve in any sport, we must step outside our comfort zones, face our fears, and take risks.

We discover this lesson as we take our first tentative steps as a baby. Of course, babies stumble and sob a lot. However, babies do not feel humiliated. Even though everyone in the room is observing them, babies do not worry about falling. But consider teens with social anxiety who fears that if they trip and fall, people will make fun of them, their parents will label them clumsy, or they could damage themselves and possibly even perish. They would avoid attempting to rise and take those awkward steps because of these ideas.

Since they would have to crawl everywhere they wanted to go—which would be embarrassing—they would likely end up staying put and taking it easy. You had to practice falling before you could walk. You have to make embarrassing blunders to feel at ease in social settings. You can either wait for those errors to occur unintentionally or deliberately cause them. Guess which technique yields the best outcomes. It is simpler than you might imagine to think up scenarios.

You might review your nervous prediction forms and devise methods to make it more likely that you will disgrace yourself. Your new exposure is there.

+ Alicia believed she was monotonous. She was hesitant to attract attention because she worried that people would judge her. How did she act? She compiled a list of dull subjects and then talked and texted about them. She deliberately cut others off.

+ Liam was concerned that he might say something foolish and look foolish. What was he doing? He placed an order for something he knew the restaurant did not offer. He also deliberately called someone by the erroneous name. He mispronounced the name of someone.

+ Bella was concerned that others would see her blushing. How did she act? Before speaking to someone or giving a presentation, she vigorously touched her cheeks. She made a lot of blush. Even if she needed to call attention to it, she ensured everyone noticed that she was blushing.

Exercise, Yoga, and Meditation: The Natural Relievers

Teens take exercise, yoga and meditation for granted, particularly when managing and living with a social anxiety disorder or any other anxiety disorder. Physical activity can help you manage social anxiety disorder or any other type of anxiety condition, reducing your risk for heart disease, high blood pressure, stroke, diabetes, and obesity.

Exercise

Moving your body is an excellent technique to manage stress and ease anxiety naturally. When you mention physical exercise, you mean any motion that causes muscles to contract. For example, your eye blinking is physical activity. Taking out the garbage is a physical task. You engage in physical activity when you eat. Exercise is a type of physical activity distinct from all others since it is more focused. Exercise is done consciously in terms of time, intensity, and movement to enhance physical strength, stamina, and cardiovascular health.

Physical activities vary, from cleaning the house to getting a bite to eat. Lifting dumbbells at the gym, jogging on the track, or swimming are some examples of exercise activities. Speaking about intensity, this word refers to how much effort you put into a task. Simply said, this is the proportion of your metabolic rate during exercise to your resting or basal metabolic rate.

There are several intensity levels of exercise. However, they are typically categorized as low, moderate, or high intensity.

There is a highly complex and nerdy approach to determining your current degree of workout intensity, but who has time for that? The talk test is the simplest yet very accurate method of selecting your current workout intensity. This is how the talk test works.

Try to converse while working out. Your exercise intensity is moderate if, with some action, you can still talk effectively. High power is when you are straining to breathe and can hardly speak. The Appropriate Intensity for Managing Anxiety The best level of exercise intensity for treating and coping with social anxiety is moderate. Why? Low intensity is far too simple to have any significant effect, such as weight loss, which can significantly boost self-esteem and lessen social anxiety.

High intensity is ineffective because it may increase tension and worsen anxiety symptoms. The last thing you need is more stress and anxiety symptoms when your goal is to manage and cope with your social anxiety effectively, is not it? Right! It is best to perform moderate exercise for at least thirty minutes three times a week. It is neither too simple to have any real influence nor too stressful to worsen your anxiety problems.

Yoga and Meditation

Yoga and meditation are the best natural relievers for anxiety and depression. Yoga and meditation are effective techniques for enhancing teens' mental health and reducing sensitivity to stress. Families can practice yoga together to reinforce ties and improve intergenerational harmony. Teenagers are more likely to utilize harmful coping techniques like substance misuse and self-harm during elevated anxiety and stress. These two relievers thus provide a beneficial substitute.

How might yoga and meditation help with anxiety?

According to research, yoga and meditation's attentive breathing and movement activate the nerves, which triggers the relaxation response. They help you to exit the sympathetic nervous system (also known as "fight or flight"). According to research, a cognitive behavioral therapy (CBT) intervention was contrasted with a CBT intervention that included yoga and meditation. Individuals noted a decrease in the physical symptoms of anxiety and panic. For individuals who used CBT in addition to yoga poses to reduce stress and anxiety, the changes were, however, more pronounced.

Yoga and Mindfulness for Anxiety

A growing body of research demonstrates how mindfulness exercises like yoga reduce stress. They teach us to observe our feelings without becoming emotionally involved. Teenagers who engage in mindfulness exercises keep their thoughts and feelings without passing judgment on them. Additionally, mindfulness training helps teenagers concentrate on the here and now. Therefore, mindfulness activities offer freedom from nagging anxieties about the future and regrets about the past.

Teen yoga helps the mind-body connection. Unfortunately, this connection is breaking more and more frequently for young people. Teenagers today tend to spend less time outdoors and consume a lot of technology. On the mat, breathing and movement coordination fosters a deeper awareness of one's interior condition and helps to repair the disconnect.

Anxiety-Relieving Yoga Breathing

Breathing space makes room in mind for stillness and focus. According to research, one of the easiest and most efficient methods for calming the nervous system is to be conscious of one's breath. Furthermore, it has a quick turnaround time.

Teens can successfully utilize breathing techniques to unwind before exams, control their temper when angry, and get a better night's sleep. Yoga breathing for anxiety, therefore, starts with the breath.

By paying attention to and managing our breathing, we can alter our thoughts and feelings. The breath can be used to manage stress and change our emotional state.

- With your feet flat, your eyes closed, and your hands at your sides, take a comfortable seat in a chair.
- Slowly inhale through your nose. Allow your chest and tummy to enlarge as your lungs fill. Try counting up to five, or however comfortable it is for you. Or concentrate on a word or phrase, such as "Breathing in."
- Use your lips or your nose to exhale whatever feels most comfortable. For example, counting can be done while exhaling. Or say something like, such as "Breathing out." Additionally, be sure that the exhalation is at least as long as the inhalation.
- Bring your attention back on the breath if you find yourself getting sidetracked.
- Repeat it for a while.

- Observe your feelings. Is your body more at ease now than it was before you began? Is your mind more relaxed?

Yoga has been demonstrated to improve feelings of connection and stress resilience. Therefore, it protects against depression. Yoga for mental health is thus being employed as an additional therapy in teen treatment facilities. Yoga also raises the levels of brain chemicals that naturally promote happiness and optimism. These substances include serotonin, enkephalins, and endorphins.

An Effective Yoga and Meditation Routine

This specific yoga posture for anxiety and despair is taken from Amy Weintraub's book Yoga for Depression. As a result, it aids in boosting energy and calming the nervous system.

- Place two folded blankets below your shoulder blades or a hard cushion under your back. As your body requires, use more or less support.
- Your head should be comfortably resting on the floor at the back by placing a rolled blanket beneath your neck.
- Put a cushion between your knees and spread your legs apart so that they are at a comfortable distance. Typically, this is around hip width.
- Allow your arms to spread at shoulder height with your palms facing up.
- Breathe and silently say, "I am." Then, say "here" aloud as you exhale, picturing the air moving to your feet.

Substance misuse has roots in despair, anxiety, and stress. Teenagers self-medicate with drugs or drink. They can avoid these damaging tendencies with healthy activities like yoga.

Yoga can thus aid in the reduction of drug and alcohol abuse. Additionally, studies have shown a connection between mindfulness and addiction rehabilitation.

In short, yoga and meditation can be powerful and successful strategies for teen mental health. It guards against depression and anxiety. Additionally, it improves self-control and well-being. Further, it enhances teen concentration and sleeping. Plus, none of these advantages has any adverse side effects. As a result, parents can introduce their children to simple yoga and meditation techniques early. As a result, as adolescents develop into teens and adults, this healthy practice will help their mental health.

Boosting Unshakable Confidence Skills

Being confident is something you can do since it comes from within. You become self-confident when you have a clear and correct perspective on life, have faith in your abilities, and fundamentally view yourself positively. It takes time and experience to increase your self-confidence. Let's find out your position.

Test Your Confidence

Read the sentences that follow one by one. Then, give yourself an honest score on a scale of 1-10.

- I can talk to anyone.
- I am ready to take on nearly any duty given to me.
- I feel comfortable with who I am.
- If I need assistance, I can ask for it.
- I assume that everyone wants to hang out with me.
- I feel at ease working at my own pace.
- Even if I do activities by myself, I can still enjoy them.
- I am not afraid to take on difficult problems.
- I feel at ease expressing my frank views.
- I do not get upset when I screw up.

How do you interpret your score?

If your score falls above 60, you have enough self-assurance. You have the self-confidence to handle almost any scenario since you know you can handle it. You can achieve your goals, take risks, act autonomously and successfully, and approach social situations without fear because of your confidence.

You become your own most extensive resource when you think you are capable and a decent, likeable person. You can better showcase your strengths if you have confidence. It also enables you to evaluate and pinpoint your areas of weakness so that, if necessary, you can strengthen these areas with the aid of outside resources. You have unwavering self-esteem because you have a positive self-perception.

Retraining your brain to shift from self-doubt to confidence is similar to building muscle through weight training in that you gradually increase the number of reps or the amount of weight over time. Finally, one can choose to have confidence. It is up to you to increase your confidence by mastering your thoughts. Remember that your perception of a circumstance affects your thoughts and behavior. Changing your doubt-based ideas is the secret to changing how you feel about yourself and behave. You can see the true image when you are confident. It is time for you to use the techniques you acquired throughout this book. Use the exercises in the next section as often as necessary as you face difficult decisions and seek to boost your confidence. You can capture your give-negative thoughts by writing down the specifics of a challenging circumstance and then use the information to replace them with go-to thoughts that lead you toward action.

Substituting Productive Behaviors for Unproductive Ones

In the future, consider utilizing one or more of the practical action alternatives listed below.

Solve a Problem: Define the issue, consider your options, balance the benefits and drawbacks, and then select a fix.

Prioritize: Avoid letting inconsequential distractions prevent you from attending to more critical matters.

Stop Using Delay Strategies: No more justifications or Diversions. Persist in your work.

Taking Baby Steps: Divide the main objective into more achievable, minor tasks.

Simply Try: Try your hardest and put in your best effort.

Use Aid: Try it on your own first, but if you require more information or assistance, use your resources.

Give Yourself Credit: Everything you do matters. Do not let fear and concern about the future stop you before you start.

Be Present and Mindful: Focus on the task and give the subject your undivided attention. You should not look on Facebook, text your buddies, or watch TV.

Stay on the Track

Like a plant, self-confidence needs fertilizer and food to take root and develop. Life's ups and downs will become less of a challenge and more of an opportunity if you make developing self-confidence an ongoing part of your daily routine. Here are some suggestions for developing healthy self-confidence.

+ Every few weeks, take the first activity to assess how you are doing.

+ Consider the emotions of grief, worry, anxiety and others as signs to pause and examine your way of thinking. Keep an eye out for instances when you emotionally, physically, or psychologically overreact; these are also occasioning to take it easy and consider your options.

+ Keep questioning your assumptions so you can compare them to the data. Work to distinguish between irrational concern and doubt.

+ Do not be terrified of unpleasant emotions. You would not get as much pleasure from the advantages without them. Your body's sensations are alerts urging you to pay attention or prepare, so do not be afraid of them.

+ Realize that you can handle any circumstance, either independently or with the aid of outside resources.

+ Try to have the most truthful, realistic, and positive perception of yourself. Recognize your ability to control your stress. Try to fulfil all of your potentials. Try something new or alter how you typically do something each day to experiment with yourself.

+ Write down the positive aspects of your life in a journal, a text, or an email to yourself. Try to think up at least five new ideas each day. You can dream and try by setting goals for yourself.

You can regularly update your confidence level by adding new or enhanced internal and external assets and resources. Use your best traits, skills, strengths, roles, and positive attributes to describe who you are. Use positive affirmations about yourself and compliments to bolster your sense of confidence. Give yourself credit for your part when positive things happen.

Keep in mind that occasionally your thoughts are accurate and might serve as a reminder to be genuinely worried. Utilizing the abilities, you have gained from this book, you will be better able to understand anxiety and take the proper, efficient course of action. You may develop unwavering self-esteem, put doubt and fear behind you, and reach your maximum potential for success and happiness by continuing to evaluate, grow, and maintain your self-confidence.

Part 3: Anxiety Disorders: Ask for Help

There are different forms of anxiety disorders: social anxiety disorder, generalized anxiety disorder, obsessive-compulsive disorder, and panic disorder. This chapter also discusses how anxiety and depression are linked. Although they differ significantly, they all share specific essential characteristics. While some teens' anxiety neatly falls into one diagnosis, for others, it may fall into two or three different classifications. Let's understand how these disorders work. List the scenarios you fear and mark each disorder that might apply to you. Ask for professional help if you think you cannot treat these disorders.

Generalized Anxiety Disorder

Emma used to worry a lot since her childhood. She fretted about many things, including a low grade in an exam jeopardizing her chances of enrolling in college. As a result, she suffered headaches and stomachaches frequently, and she felt stressed out almost all the time. Things were truly bad when there was nothing to keep her from worrying at night. Her mind was spinning endlessly. She frequently struggled to fall asleep, and when she did, she woke up cranky and fatigued from being restless all night.

Emma suffers from a generalized anxiety disorder. She is worried about being judged or having a panic attack. Teens with general anxiety worry about their studies, families, jobs, health, and global events.

There are three basic questions to know if you have been suffering from generalized anxiety disorder:

What am I frightened of?

_____

_____

_____

What is the worst that might occur?

_____

_____

_____

What does this indicate about me, my life, or what is ahead?

_____

_____

_____

The Right Approach

Emma's test grades were as impressive as she had planned. Although upset, she did not start fretting again about getting into a good college. She could focus on learning the new information she received in the lesson. She knew she had done everything she could to prepare herself by studying. She had no control over her grades; her teacher determined them. You can break the cycle of avoidance when you accept the worry that comes with not knowing how things will turn out. Your life is now a minefield where you have to worry over everything you want to do. You deserve to live your ideal life without having to worry needlessly. Why are you holding out?

Panic Attacks

Alicia felt that someone was hard-squeezing her. She was having problems breathing, felt lightheaded and dizzy, and thought her heart might be racing out of her chest. Her parents responded to her call, picked her up, and drove her to the hospital's emergency room. The physician informed her that she was experiencing a panic attack and was in good health.

She was relieved when Alicia was informed that there was nothing wrong with her. She felt normal until some weeks later when she experienced another panic attack while seated in her classroom. The knowledge that nothing was wrong did not make her feel any less concerned. She was so dizzy that she was worried she would pass out or somehow lose control. She could stand up and leave the classroom while expressing her discomfort to the teacher.

She then called her mother to arrange an immediate pickup. The following day, her mother scheduled a consultation with Alicia's physician to see if there was anything they could do. Alicia was given medication by the physician to use in case she experienced another panic attack.

She was constantly concerned that she might have another attack whenever her heart rate rose, and occasionally she did. Alicia took a tablet as soon as she began to experience the symptoms, which typically prevented her from experiencing a full-blown panic attack.

The first step to controlling panic attacks is to pinpoint the anxious thoughts or monkey mind interpretations that have been setting off your panic episodes because they are not caused by the environment or your physical sensations but rather by how you perceive them. For example, you have probably noticed that our breathing gets shallow and quick when we're anxious. Physical sensations become more intense as a result of this type of breathing, which causes physiological changes as well as the consequence of making you breathe more quickly and shallowly.

Breathing in this manner, you are letting your body know that you are signaling to your mind that there is a problem. Instead of fighting your feelings of anxiety, try breathing the opposite way:

- Breathe in, fill your lungs and allow your belly to soften and expand.
- Completely exhale so that your belly tightens.
- Reiterate carefully and purposefully.

Your body will know you can handle this by telling it to breathe gently and steadily. You can endure the powerful and painful surges of sensation by breathing in this way.

Alicia exerted a lot of effort to tame her panic attacks. Within a year, her fear of having a panic attack had decreased. She could identify the waves of anxiety she experienced as being harmless. She still did not like them, but they no longer frightened her as they had. She was therefore experiencing significantly fewer panic attacks. In actuality, they no longer felt much like panic attacks. They were softer and scarcer, as well as more numerous.

She identified her anxious thoughts, wrote down her catastrophizing thoughts, and then replaced them with alternative thoughts. This strategy gave her a choice to respond based on facts or her fear.

Obsessive Compulsive Disorder

Lucia was regarded as a perfectionist. Her books, clothes, and papers were always in order. She preferred it this way, and it was not problematic. But suddenly, things started to spiral out of control. She was reading for class when she began questioning whether or not she truly understood what she had just read. As a result, she proceeded to reread everything. She began altering and removing sections of her reports that did not seem to go together correctly. She repeatedly checked her classroom, locker, and car out of concern that she might have forgotten to bring something crucial. She repeatedly double-checked her bag to make sure it included everything. Though she found this constant monitoring annoying and upsetting, Lucia struggled to fight the temptation.

Lucia was suffering from obsessive-compulsive disorder (OCD). OCD is thoughts present in the form of obsessions and compulsions.

+ Obsessions with OCD are unwanted intrusive thoughts, ideas, or desires that make you feel anxious and distressed. Even if you have these ideas, they are not very logical. Obsessive-compulsive thoughts lead to making irrational assumptions.
+ OCD compulsions are behaviors you feel you must perform by rigid rules to stop the events you are constantly thinking about from occurring. Due to the intense drive the OCD sufferer experiences to perform these actions, they are regarded as compulsive behaviors. In addition, because they take up more time

than you would want, they diverge from a typical routine.

Lucia's Obsession: What if I forgot something crucial, skipped an assignment, and received a poor mark? I might feel awful forever if things are not perfect.

Repeatedly check your backpack to ensure you haven't forgotten or abandoned anything. Keep your space tidy so that you can unwind. Your irrational reasoning holds that you are safe and do not forget anything because you check and double-check your backpack and keep your room tidy.

Tools to Control OCD

Treating your obsessive thoughts as inconsequential and your compulsive rituals as needless is the only way to prevent OCD from taking over your life. How can you disregard your obsessive thoughts? Simply by exposing yourself to them and ceasing to shun them. You can argue," how can I do this as I am constantly exposed to obsessive thoughts." This is not true. You have been attempting to stay away from anything or any setting that can set off the thoughts because you haven't been able to manage the thoughts themselves. And if that is not possible, you have attempted to stop worrying about the urges making you do them.

Your irrational reasoning will alter after you accept your anxiety and allow yourself to feel it. It will appear more like you have accepted the idea and are secure. The idea cannot possibly be so harmful after all. That kind of approach can be tolerated without sacrificing one's aspirations. Of course, there will always be a minuscule possibility that a terrifying concept will come true. Life will always include some danger. But I am confident you will discover that putting up with some uncertainty is preferable to having OCD.

Depression

Teens frequently suffer from both anxiety and depression. This is because there is a causal connection between the two. As you have seen in this book, your mind will constantly think up excuses for why you should not do anything while you are feeling anxious. Over time, you lose faith in your ability to accomplish things when you repeatedly put off tasks you sincerely desire to complete—having no hope and feeling helpless.

The hallmark of depression is a lack of motivation. For instance, if your social anxiety prevents you from attending parties or other social gatherings, you can start to think, "I will never make friends or have a girlfriend or boyfriend." You might believe I will have to live here with my parents and work a terrible job forever if I do not go on excursions or to events where there are many people because of my anxiety or agoraphobia. You are not doing the things that would make you feel better if you are too exhausted, nervous, or unmotivated.

You get even more tense, worn out, and uninspired. When you avoid doing things that can improve your mood, you risk becoming even more unhappy and lacking motivation. The central theme of this book is taking control of your life by overcoming your anxieties. Your depression might disappear if you do the activities in this book to deal with your anxiety. Getting the depressed individual to resume the activities she quit because she lacked motivation is one method of treating depression. Everyone is familiar with the idea that inspiration inspires action. The opposite is true if you are depressed: motivation comes from action (which leads to more effort).

Motivation and action go hand in hand, like hunger and food. You eat because you are hungry. You keep alive through eating, and someday you will become hungry again. When someone is ill and does not feel like eating, they are frequently urged to eat because the food would help them regain their strength. You must start the cycle of motivation by acting even when you do not feel like it to feel motivated.

Choose a task you have previously found enjoyable or would like to complete but lack the motivation to undertake. It could involve physical exercises like riding a bike, sketching, or dancing. Another example might be completing your homework or cleaning your room. No matter how exhausted or unmotivated you feel, do it, whatever it is. However, you might discover that you feel slightly more inspired to carry on after committing to anything for just some days.

Teenagers who are depressed can consider suicide or even plan to do so. You must get help if you are considering suicide. Suicide is a long-term solution to a short-term issue. Regardless of how awful you may feel right now, things will improve. Share your feelings and views with others. Call a crisis hotline, speak with your school counselor, or tell a parent or friend. This applies to all adolescents who are depressed.

Getting assistance is usually a good idea. Depression can be successfully treated with both counseling and medicine. Most individuals recall their adolescence as a challenging period due to physical changes, peer and academic pressure, and the impending demands of adulthood. You might struggle more than most teens, especially if you are nervous.

Remember that you are not alone, and it is worth fighting for your life because it is significant. Depression may be conquered, just like anxiety. Unbelievably, there is an additional reward for overcoming depression and anxiety. No life is without failures and disappointments. Thus, learning how to ignite your motivation by acting will be very helpful throughout your life. You can utilize every strategy you know in this book for the rest of your life to accomplish your goals and go to your desired places. So why are you still waiting? It is time to act now.

Find a Professional Therapist

Find a therapist who should make you feel at ease. You have every right to inquire about the therapist you are considering to ensure they are a suitable fit for you and have experience with the problems you want to address. The following set of questions will help you select a therapist who can assist you:

- What kind of cognitive behavioral therapy training does he have?
- What experience does he have with treating anxiety?
- What percentage of their present patient base is treated for anxiety?
- Do you think his efforts to treat anxiety have been successful?
- What methods does he employ to combat anxiety?
- Do you find it easier to recognize unhelpful ideas and actions to help you face your anxieties using these techniques?
- Is he prepared to leave his desk if necessary to assist him in facing his fears?

Regarding Medicine

You might wish to discuss medication if your severe anxiety is interfering with your ability to carry out daily tasks like leaving the house to attend class or completing the exercises in this book. Family doctors, general practitioners, or psychiatrists typically prescribe anxiety medication (medical doctors specializing in mental health). People who use the medication in conjunction with CBT see the best benefits among those who do so. This is logical. While the treatment gives you the tools to manage anxiety now and in the future, the medication can help you feel less anxious overall. This will make it much less probable for your anxiety to resurface when you stop taking your medicine. On the other hand, when you stop taking your medication, your anxiety will likely return if you only rely on it.

A Goodbye Note

We frequently believe that we are the only ones experiencing anxiety. While everyone else seems strong and confident, we believe we are broken. That is untrue. Almost everyone has anxiety at some point. Some people are frightened of heights, while others worry about many issues. Others have anxiety before public speaking engagements or when they meet new people.

We have a lot of knowledge about how to deal with anxiety. Most people can get over their anxiety with the aid of cognitive behavioral therapy (CBT), a type of psychological treatment. Research on how emotions function and what people may do to feel better is the foundation of CBT. CBT gives people tools to combat depression, anxiety, and many other problems. Although learning these talents takes practice, everyone can do it. This book filled that need.

It explains and demonstrates how to get rid of social anxiety. This book can help you get over your social anxiety and feel much better if you complete the worksheets and do the experiments suggested. You could feel anxious during some of the activities. This is advantageous since we know that fear only diminishes when we confront it rather than run away from it. I outlined simple steps you can take to boost your confidence to make it easier for you.

This book is typically written for grown-ups. It is unfortunate because teenagers frequently experience higher levels of anxiety than adults. That is why I was delighted to write this book just for you. Small steps can guide you to worthwhile places when you have a map. This book serves as a guide if you are anxious around others. By doing it slowly, you can undertake things that frighten you.